LEARNING TO LEARN
Developing study skills with pupils who have special educational needs

GORDON MALONE

and

DOROTHY SMITH

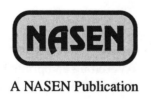

A NASEN Publication

Published in 1996

ISBN 0 906730 79 1

Published by NASEN Enterprises Ltd.
NASEN Enterprises is a company limited by guarantee, registered in England and Wales. Company No. 2637438.

Further copies of this book and details of NASEN's many other publications may be obtained from the Publications Department at its registered office: NASEN House, 4/5 Amber Business Village, Amber Close, Amington, Tamworth, Staffs. B77 4RP.
Tel: 01827 311500; Fax: 01827 313005;
email: nasen@bbcnc.org.uk.

Copy editing by Nicola von Schreiber.
Cover design by Graphic Images.
Typeset in Times by J. C. Typesetting and printed in the United Kingdom by J. H. Brookes Ltd, Stoke-on-Trent.

LEARNING TO LEARN
Developing study skills with pupils who have special educational needs

Contents

Acknowledgements

The Authors and Publishers wish to express their gratitude to:

- members of NASEN's Publications Sub-Committee for their helpful comments;
- Frances James, Advisory Headteacher for Learning Support, Suffolk, for her contribution on the section about Information Technology.

Introduction

There are well over a hundred books about study skills. Most of them attempt to cover the needs of students in higher or further education and are self-help manuals. Good examples of these are published by the Open University. There are relatively few books on helping pupils in schools to develop learning skills, although *Encouraging Classroom Success* (Ainscow and Tweddle, 1988) advocates '...the ultimate goal is to help pupils take responsibility for their own learning.' *Improving Study Skills* (Selmes, 1987) describes in some detail an attempt to develop and encourage the teaching of study skills in some secondary schools in Scotland.

In particular, there seems to be no publication aimed specifically at the needs of children with special educational needs.

The purpose of this book is to consider to what extent pupils with special educational needs in mainstream schools can be helped to *learn to learn* with the emphasis placed not so much on *what* is to be learned as on *the processes of learning,* and how teachers can help pupils to develop and improve their learning skills. It is about *metacognition,* which is the process of learning how to learn by reflecting upon how one learns as an individual. Unless a pupil wants to learn, sees the point of it and positively enjoys it, the task of the teacher can become very difficult and unrewarding.

Learning to learn is a matter of asking the right questions, knowing where to look for information and how to process it and who to ask for help. It is about working effectively, knowing the best ways to establish facts in the long-term memory and what to do when faced with a failure to understand something.

It follows that the task of the teacher is to help pupils to ask the right questions, to direct them to sources of information, occasionally providing it themselves. It involves getting accepted as a mentor and guide and entering into the thought processes of pupils in order to discover what learning strategies are being attempted and extending these strategies in order to lead pupils to effective learning techniques.

The approach adopted in this book is based on the assumptions that the role of a teacher is to provide learning opportunities, and that there is more to this than the presentation of facts and ideas for absorption by the pupil.

This book focuses on the problems pupils might face when they are in Year 5 upwards and, therefore, it is applicable to teachers in the later primary years and all the secondary years. The ideas suggested may have some

5

relevance for those pupils in special schools or units, but the authors' intention is for guidance to be given for pupils requiring help with study skills in the mainstream classroom. Although its main concern is for those pupils who have been designated as having special educational needs, the publication will have some application for all mainstream teachers and their pupils.

It is intended that this book should give practical advice and, therefore, it is not an 'academic' work. Each area is briefly introduced but the main content is the suggestions for teachers and parents. Some actual examples are, therefore, placed within the text. The following case studies are based on the learning problems of actual pupils (their names have been changed).

John

John is 12 years old and is in Year 7. Primary records show that some concern was felt about his learning difficulties when he was younger. In those primary years his reading and spelling skills were targeted and because of this his attainments in these areas reached a functional level of around 10 years. It was felt that he could access the secondary curriculum without undue problems. After a few weeks subject teachers became worried about John's work.

Identified problems were:

- homework forgotten or not completed satisfactorily;

- minimum output of work achieved in lessons;

- apparent misunderstanding of instructions.

After observation of John in lessons it was found that although he could read, understand and spell what was expected of him, his auditory memory powers were so weak that he could not remember, process and recall any information that was needed in this auditory mode. Given a sentence of about six to ten words he would forget the beginning words. These memory problems had great implications where curriculum accessing was concerned. If John couldn't remember, process and recall, he could not do homework, nor could he complete his work. He was being penalised for something out of his control.

To help John his subject teachers were asked to:

- make as much of his work as visual as possible. Instructions should be written or diagrammatic so that he had points of reference;

- write homework instructions for him in his homework diary and arrange for a mentor to check that he knew what work was expected of him;

- liaise with his parents so that they would check his homework and help him when necessary;

- arrange that his mentor would check his homework after he had completed it;

- give him short achievable tasks to undertake in class and check with him that he was coping;

- monitor his progress to see if he was becoming more proficient at keeping on task;

- involve him with his own learning.

After a few weeks a noticeable change occurred in John's learning styles and work output. His subject teachers made sure that he knew what to do in lessons and a teacher from the special needs department was given the task of becoming John's mentor. John learnt to report to her at the end of each day for a short discussion about his homework and for a longer session during one PSE lesson. John's parents liaised regularly with the school.

Sam

Sam is 10 years old and is in Year 5. He has a statement of special educational needs because of specific learning difficulties. Sam does not read nor does he spell. In fact, he is unable to score on any standardised reading and spelling test although his IQ has been measured as above average. He is very articulate and has good, but patchy, general knowledge. Sam's auditory and visual memory processes are particularly limited which means learning by conventional methods is very difficult. He has additional teaching support hours which give him a daily input of a multi-sensory literacy programme. This appears to have little impact.

It is in the classroom that Sam has most difficulties. Because he cannot read or record in the conventional way, he cannot access the curriculum. Because he cannot remember instructions and information, he tends to lose track of what is going on and consequently Sam's behaviour is deteriorating.

In order to help Sam the following suggestions were given:

- arrange for additional ancillary support help to be given when written work is required so that he can dictate his work which then can be word processed by the ancillary for good presentation;

- for the future this dictation will also be given on cassette or dictaphone;

- any written work should be read back to Sam so that he can try to recall and read what he has dictated and be able to illustrate etc.;

- so that he can start to organise his thoughts he should be helped to brainstorm key words which will then form the basis of a reading programme to help him to recall key topic words;

- some work will be cassette-recorded for him so that he can play this over to gain the required information;

- some worksheets will be illustrated or arranged in diagrammatic form so that he has visual clues.

Sam found it easier to learn the subject specific words when these were presented with a symbol or picture to jog his memory. He soon was able to cope with simplified worksheets. He learnt to use a dictaphone for recording work and his class teacher was able to listen to this and judge what he had learnt. The structured literacy programme was suspended until it was thought that Sam could cope and his support teacher took over the in-class support for project completion, especially in science and history which Sam excelled in. The ancillary support put information on tape and built up both tape and worksheet resources under the class teacher's direction. Because Sam was becoming more successful his behaviour started improving.

8

Adrian

Adrian is 17 years old and is in the Lower Sixth. He wants to become involved in drama and is, therefore, taking English and drama at 'A' level. However, his English GCSE grade was a bare 'C' and his teachers find that, although orally he is very competent and he can comprehend all the texts that are required, he cannot write essays which make any sense. He writes in a jumble of thoughts with no introduction, paragraphs which link or conclusions.

In order to help Adrian the following suggestions were given:

- in order to learn how to write essays competently Adrian should talk through his ideas about the given title and an adult would write these down using keywords and phrases;

- Adrian should be encouraged to read these and underline using different colours those that go together;

- these should be discussed and altered with help if need be;

- he should choose a beginning and write these in two to three sentences;

- with help he should choose a group which came first in the theme and weave these into a paragraph;

- a similar procedure should take place with subsequent paragraphs and the conclusion;

- the adult would read his essay out loud so that Adrian could hear if it made sense and hear if he had anything else to say which could be inserted;

- the second essay should be undertaken by Adrian with his own brainstorming and groupings but before he would start writing these would be checked by the adult;

- he would be encouraged to draft and redraft (especially if he could word process so that the 'cut and paste' facility could be used);

- he would continue with help until it was felt that he was becoming more competent at producing logically written essays.

The co-ordinator of special educational needs worked with Adrian twice a week, once at lunchtime and once when Adrian had a study period. She liaised with his English teacher and between them they helped Adrian to write essays that began to show structure. The next objective would be to help him with examination techniques and give him some essays to complete under timed conditions.

Chapter 1 - Teaching approaches

Learning in school usually takes place within the context of a classroom and under the supervision or control of a teacher. What a pupil learns depends on how this teacher approaches his or her subject.

Process-teaching

In the context of the development of learning skills the *way* things are taught or presented is more important than the content, because the way things are taught has a great deal to do with the development of attitudes, motivation and self-confidence.

In this chapter the concept of the pupil as an independent or self-directed learner is introduced, which will be constantly referred to throughout the book. First it has to be acknowledged by both teacher and learner that there can be difficulties when learning takes place. Then it has to be accepted that these difficulties can be overcome once they are understood and correctly helped. The partnership of teacher and learner will then be ready to assist learning towards self-direction. Teachers need to structure work to produce success for all their pupils.

The process model of the curriculum considers desirable outcomes or qualities and asks what teaching and learning behaviours are likely to foster and develop them.

Qualities of self-directed learners include:

- *good motivation;*

- an *interest* and an *enjoyment* in whatever is being studied;

- *self-confidence* – believing that whatever they are doing is good and worth the effort;

- *success.*

If pupils are to enjoy their work, to be confident and successful, what can the teacher do towards this end? This is a question which is central to the message of this book.

Pupils who are successful gain in confidence. Successful and confident pupils almost always turn out to be well motivated. The task of the teacher in this regard is to protect his or her pupils from failure, to underline success with frequent but justified praise and to structure work to produce success for all pupils.

It is important that pupils should be aware of where a particular difficulty lies and how they and their teachers are going to provide ways to help it. Teachers should be aware of patterns in their pupils' learning behaviours so that they know when work seems to be progressing well and when there is a problem. This can be undertaken by observation in the classroom and by questioning the learner. It is at the point where learning breaks down that help should be given, either ways of learning the particular problem area or strategies to circumvent this.

Problem solving

Some subjects can be taught by the application of a problem solving approach. Learning itself is largely about problem solving and discovering ways to do it. Each subject discipline might be regarded as a set of problems and approaches to solving them.

A problem solving approach is a good way to encourage pupil involvement. Before pupils are presented with a problem, they *must be able to understand and process that problem and possess the knowledge and understanding to solve it.* Problem solving involves applying existing knowledge in new contexts.

The process of problem solving requires:

- a clear statement of the problem;

- a looking ahead to see what the problem may look like when it is solved;

- an identification of the main factors within this so that the less relevant factors can be put into perspective;

- thinking about known knowledge which might be helpful in solving the problem;

- a strategy for solving it (which in practice may mean preparing several plans and choosing between them);

11

- carrying out the chosen strategy and reaching conclusions;

- evaluating the procedure adopted and the validity of the conclusions reached.

Problem solving approach – an example

In the science section it is interesting that the National Curriculum lists facts and ideas under the words 'pupils should be taught'. This can and often does imply simply *telling* and this can be a convenient way of teaching, especially if classes are big, but is not very effective and certainly does not encourage thinking.

In the general introduction to each Programme of Study are the words 'Pupils should be given opportunities to:
ask questions ...
use focussed exploration ...
use firsthand experience ...' etc.

These *opportunities* are perhaps best provided through a problem solving approach.
e.g. (from Key Stage 2 material and their properties 1a)
'Compare everyday materials, e.g. wood, rock, iron, aluminium, paper, polythene on the basis of their properties ... hardness, strength, flexibility ...'

The problem solving approach requires the use of open-ended questions, which can start very open ended and then become more focussed as necessary. The lesson would start with the identification of the materials to be investigated.
e.g. Here are some materials. Can you name them? (Closed question.)
Now what could we find out about these materials? (Each group to write out five or six ideas.)
How could we compare how *hard* they are? (Each group to write down their ideas.)
How could we compare how *strong* they are? Just what do we mean by strong? (Closed question.)
How could we compare how *flexible* they are? What does flexible mean? (Closed question.)
How can we be *fair* when we carry out these tests? etc.

The teacher of a self-motivated learner

If teachers take on this approach, then there has to be a change of emphasis from the teacher as expert in a particular subject passing on his or her knowledge, to that of expert in learning or rather expert in helping pupils to learn. Subject expertise takes very much a secondary place. The skills of the teacher are those of a *mentor,* of understanding how pupils think and how pupils learn and applying such knowledge and skills to individual pupils rather than to classes of pupils.

Much depends on the enthusiasm of the teacher and how this is relayed to the learners. Children need an environment that provides opportunities for learning. They should be encouraged to make enquiries for themselves. They need opportunities for *structured* directed work and guided discovery learning (a balance between formal teaching and utilising children's natural energies and interests for their own learning). Pupils will be better motivated and more involved in their own learning if they are discovering things for themselves than if they are simply told what to do. The task of the teacher is to provide opportunities for discoveries to occur, to arrange these happenings in some sensible order and to keep a record of the attainment or achievement of each pupil.

It is not the place of this book to discuss classroom organisation. However, it should be stressed that discovery learning can take place in what appears to be a highly structured and ordered environment.

Most educational ideas work beautifully with single pupils. (The classic example is Rousseau's *Emile.*) Given a large class, salvation comes from providing work that keeps all the pupils busy most of the time. In this context working with individual pupils in order to encourage them to take more responsibility for their own learning is far from easy. The more pupils that do just that, however, the easier it becomes to cope with the rest.

Differentiation

'Differentiation' is quoted in National Curriculum documents and in the Code of Practice. It is a term that is frequently used and a process much to be recommended but one that is difficult to put into practice. Visser defined differentiation as:

'... the process whereby the teachers meet the need for progress through the curriculum by selecting appropriate teaching methods to match an individual child's learning strategies, within a group situation.'

(Visser, 1993)

The *Code of Practice on the Identification and Assessment of Special Educational Needs* (DfE 1994) requires some kind of differentiated teaching and learning to take place when pupils are placed on the first stage of the assessment process. Because pupils have differing aptitudes and abilities whole class teaching has limited applicability. Teachers need to be aware of how to choose appropriate teaching methods for any particular child with learning difficulties. This, in turn, means that teachers must know how the child learns and what difficulties that child experiences in learning. This knowledge can be gained by close observation of how the child tackles or attempts any particular learning task. At this stage formal individual assessment and interview should not be necessary.

In *Differentiation: Your Responsibility* (Barthorpe and Visser, 1991), the authors list possible areas for consideration where differentiation is concerned. These give some general indicators for teachers. In this book each chapter includes some consideration of differentiation.

The point of differentiation is to allow each pupil to work at his or her own level or pace. It is to stretch the most able and to ensure that the less able does not get lost. Sometimes differentiation can be achieved simply by allowing all children to enjoy an identical experience, but allowing and expecting different responses from them.

Differentiated worksheets are another approach. The differentiation provided by this means includes the possibility of allowing for different starting points, more and simpler steps, different words and different responses. A danger to be avoided is the suggestion that clever children do one set and less clever children do another. This highlights one of the problems of classroom organisation.

Perhaps a solution would be to arrange groups so that they each contain children across the whole ability range, and provide the group with a set of differentiated worksheets, and they have to choose which to use. Or maybe a single worksheet can include a common core which is pitched at the level of the child with the greatest learning difficulties, but goes on to provide more demanding tasks for the more able.

Examples

(Science National Curriculum Key Stage 2 1d)
Describe and group rocks and soils on the basis of characteristics, including appearance, texture and permeability.

Worksheet A (for the most able)
You are provided with ten labelled rock samples.
Make a suitable table and record the appearance, texture and permeability
of each sample.

Worksheet B
Here are ten rock samples.
Each one has a name on it.
Look at them carefully and fill in the chart. One has been filled in to
help you.

Appearance = what the rock looks like.
Texture = what the rock feels like.
Permeability = does the rock let water soak through it?

To test for permeability hold the rock so that it just touches the surface
of some water in a bowl.
Does the water soak up into the rock?

Rock	Appearance	Texture	Permeability
Quartz	clear colourless crystalline	smooth like glass	not permeable
Limestone			
Malachite			
Chalk			

Worksheet C
Look at the bits of rock.
Fill in the spaces below using words from the list. (One has been done for you.)

Name of Rock	What does it look like?	Is it rough or smooth?	Does it soak up water?
Chalk	white solid lump	rough	a bit
Limestone			
etc.			

Words to use
Colours: white, green, brown, black, shiny, etc.

Worksheet D
Not on paper at all, but recorded on cassette. A table for completion is available on a computer. Pupils have to identify appropriate responses from lists provided.

Chapter 2 - Special educational needs

The *Education Act 1993* defines special educational needs as follows: 'A child has special educational needs if he or she has a learning difficulty which calls for special educational provision to be made for him or her. A child has a learning difficulty if he or she ... has a significantly greater difficulty in learning than the majority of children of the same age.' This is repeated in the Code of Practice with special educational needs being equated with learning difficulties.

There are pupils in every class who may have problems accessing the curriculum. These children have learning difficulties which may require changes in teaching style and approaches and an awareness that children learn in different ways. If it is found that any child has a problem in learning because he or she lacks appropriate study skills then teachers will need to address this issue.

This book provides suggestions for teachers and/or parents of pupils in mainstream schools who have learning difficulties which may be labelled as moderate, mild or specific. Some pupils will have general all-round learning problems which affect all or nearly all the areas of the curriculum. Other pupils will have learning difficulties in a few areas especially if those pupils are dyslexic where their problems in the literacy areas are apparent. Often these pupils will have organisational and memory difficulties.

No particular mention will be made in this book of pupils with behavioural problems. However, it should be mentioned in this section that many pupils misbehave in certain lessons because they have difficulties in accessing these curriculum areas. Because they do not understand, because they cannot process information, because they do not possess the correct skills for learning these pupils vote with their feet and their voices. Not all of these unacceptable behaviour problems can be helped by providing a more suitable learning environment and aids for learning but these should be tried. All pupils have a right to learn.

The Code of Practice outlines a staged process on identification and assessment. Schools will have their own policies and within these there will be processes outlined which teachers will follow when pupils are deemed to have a learning difficulty. However, teachers should not wait for labelling of pupils to take place in order to act if they feel that action is necessary.

The Code stresses the importance of parental involvement and partnership. The parents/carers of any child who is identified as having special educational needs and is placed on the first level of the staged process have to be informed. Parents must be told about the type of help and support given to their children. It is hoped that the parents will continue this help at home wherever possible. Within this book parents are mentioned specifically in Chapter 5 but parents should be involved and made aware of any changes in teaching which concerns their children. The Code also states that the children themselves should be involved. Often children can take much responsibility for their own learning if they are given help in understanding what their 'problems' are. This, in fact, is the principle purpose of this book!

Chapter 3 - Barriers to effective study skills and how to overcome them

Children differ in aptitudes, abilities, self-esteem, and motivation and in the ways they approach their learning. Although the authors do not wish to discuss the notion of intelligence we feel that there are often some elements within the child which either help or hinder them to understand concepts etc. which are a barrier to learning. Often these cannot be rectified and, therefore, the pupils will need alternative strategies in order to learn as effectively as their peers. Those pupils who are well into the staged approach of the Code of Practice mentioned in Chapter 2 or who have been made subject to a statement may have had their 'intelligence' measured with an IQ test. This can only be helpful if used as a guide when teachers decide on the best way of helping the pupil access the curriculum. As measures of cognitive ability IQ scores can change over time.

Receptive language

Receptive language is the ability to take in and understand the spoken or written word. Failure to understand what is read or being said could be a result of poor listening skills, if having switched off through boredom or because the material being presented is too complex. There is also the possibility that the child may have some type of hearing problem. Often it is difficult for the subject teacher to know whether a seemingly non-motivated pupil or one who displays low-level behavioural problems is able to understand the language presented in the classroom. Pupils with special educational needs may have been assessed by co-ordinators of special needs, advisory teachers or educational psychologists who would have been able to determine their receptive language abilities. This information should be readily available to all teachers. School nurses, doctors or specialist advisory teachers for the hearing impaired can be asked to check hearing. When pupils feel confident to ask if they don't understand something, their teachers will then be able to give the help needed. If teachers suspect that a pupil is finding the language of the classroom a problem they should either talk to the pupil individually so as not to make an issue of the difficulty or seek advice from the special needs staff.

Within the classroom teachers can help by:

- monitoring printed material in order to make sure that it does not exceed pupils' language understanding;

- being constantly aware of their own use of language so that pupils both understand what is being stated and also can gain language enrichment;

- helping the pupils to understand by repeating information or instructions in a simplified way;

- backing up oral information or instructions by written material or by drawings or diagrams;

- allowing pupils plenty of time to think and time to reply to questions;

- checking that the pupils understand by allowing them to explain the information or instructions in their own words;

- reorganising the seating position for pupils suspected of having some kind of hearing loss.

Expressive language

Expressive language is the production of words. Expressive language difficulties are problems which show themselves in pupils lacking the ability to express themselves clearly and appropriately. They may have an extremely limited general vocabulary and make inappropriate use of subject specific vocabulary. As a result they may be understandably reluctant to express themselves orally or in writing. Conversational language is visual in that it occurs through direct experience and is context bound. Academic language is far more abstract as it is removed from what is known and experienced. It contains much new vocabulary. Pupils with learning difficulties may cope with conversational language but will have problems with the language of the classroom. As with receptive language problems some pupils with special educational needs may have been assessed and staff should be given any appropriate information although it is far more difficult to assess expressive language.

> **In the classroom teachers can help by:**
>
> - developing confidence, accepting and praising all honest effort;
>
> - providing opportunities for discussion in groups and pairs, so that pupils can practise expressing themselves in a non-threatening environment;
>
> - helping pupils to extend their vocabulary by explanations and word activities;
>
> - allowing the pupils to know what they have to talk about in advance so that they are able to practise;
>
> - using 'Circle time' activities.

Understanding

Many difficulties related to receptive and expressive language are a result of limited understanding and they also result in the pupils experiencing limited understanding. Understanding, concepts and language are intimately related and central to all learning and teaching.

> **In the classroom teachers can help by:**
>
> - accepting that *teacher explanation* is only a part of the process of developing understanding. It so often doesn't work!
>
> - providing experiences that enable concepts to be developed;
>
> - encouraging lots of discussion so that the use of new ideas and the words that go with them may be practised and tested on others. This is one of the main advantages of group work.

Memory

Three types of memory are usually recognised: short-term, acting working memory and long-term. We use short-term memory when we remember a telephone number just long enough to dial it and then we immediately forget it. Acting working memory is the intermediate memory between short-term and long-term memories. A needed item can be stored here while other pieces of relevant information are used first and then when it is required this stored item can be retrieved and utilised. However, this item can easily be dislodged. We also use information from the working memory for transference into long-term memory. Information which is stored in long-term memory is needed for such events as tests and examinations.

Memories can work in both the visual and the auditory modes and some pupils find it easier to use their visual recall than their auditory recall. Others are the opposite. If it is known that pupils can cope with visual clueing, visual processing, visual retention and visual recall rather than the auditory side, they should be helped to access the curriculum by being given visual clues. These pupils will find it difficult to retain information that is presented orally but will find it easier to copy notes and use reading and diagrammatic material to aid their awareness. (Of course, they have to have adequate reading attainments.) Those pupils whose auditory memories are stronger will find it easier to cope within the classroom where the spoken word is often used but they will find it more difficult to read silently and recall or to work from maps or diagrams. However, there are some pupils whose visual and auditory memories are particularly weak and who will need very well-organised strategies for coping.

Two aspects of long-term memory are that which is the result of rote learning and that which is dependent on understanding. There is, of course, no clear dividing line between the two, and often rote learning can be facilitated by understanding if the matter to be learnt can be systematised or classified in some way. Rote learning can be used by pupils as a substitute for understanding, a strategy that is very harmful to good learning because it can involve an avoidance of understanding, as well as a great deal of wasted time.

As with receptive language problems it is sometimes difficult for the teacher to recognise the pupil with memory difficulties as their behaviours may appear to be the result of inattentiveness, lack of concentration or poor receptive understanding skills. These pupils often fail to complete tasks satisfactorily, forget to do their homework and are unable to take messages. They are pupils with genuine memory problems who cannot easily retain information, process it and utilise it. They may forget the beginning of a sentence before the end is given. Sometimes problems can be reduced by choosing an alternative route or by simple avoidance of the need for memorising. The requirement that pupils should memorise things should be kept to a minimum, and alternatives used whenever possible.

The teacher's role in relation to memory is in deciding what is to be memorised and in what order, as well as justifying and, whenever possible, reducing the drudgery involved. If there are processes which need to be learnt automatically by memory then these have to be practised daily and so it is important to make sure that the parents and child will work together on these.

In the classroom teachers can help by:

- repeating information and breaking instructions down into very small steps;

- relating the memory requirement to the pupil concerned;

- getting the pupils to repeat or rehearse what has to be done or making sure this is recorded in other ways;

- reviewing the range of audio-visual aids that can be used. One such aid here could be that information is placed on cassette so that the pupils control their own rate of listening;

- reviewing the amount of listening required. If the teacher allows the pupils to read and answer rather than listen and answer this will also alleviate any strain on the working memory;

- giving the questions first so these can be looked out for before the passage is read. This reading would be best done by the pupils if they are capable of this. This could be very useful where subject specific information is required;

- expanding memory skills by giving messages or information which are increased in length and complexity as time goes on;

- helping pupils to find logical ways of grouping items into subgroups if there are problems with remembering lists. Telephone and other numbers can be grouped as can other information;

- giving techniques such as repeating the information silently or making very simple notes;

- providing some kind of *aide-mémoire* such as some written headings;

- providing for those pupils who need them relevant lists, crib sheets, table sheets and lists of dates for reference purposes;

- telling pupils when they are about to say something that has to be remembered;

- telling pupils what will be told them and after telling them tell them again what has been said;

- giving more time if that is what is needed. This has implications for when the pupils take internal and external examinations.

Motivation

Providing motivation is about developing interest and involvement. Thus this is why discovery learning and problem solving can be important. Possibly the best motivator is success. Self-satisfaction is important, but the teacher has an important role in fostering this.

In the classroom teachers can help by:

- ensuring that success is gained and recognised and praised accordingly;

- providing some tasks that stretch but do not provide insurmountable difficulties. Some work should be seen as easy!

- providing tasks for some pupils that are short and easily achievable;

- remembering that there is a need to provide relaxation and enjoyment within any course of study;

- sharing the purpose of each lesson and explaining the long-term aims to all pupils;

- recognising when success is not being achieved and being able to change the immediate targets so that interest is sustained.

The need for 'learning readiness'

'Learning readiness' as used here does not imply that one has to wait for a child to become 'ready' to be taught a particular process but rather that teachers should be aware of what is needed by the learner before that process is understood and consolidated. In a subject which relies on some sequential learning there is no point in attempting to introduce ideas that require for their understanding earlier concepts which have not yet been developed.

Have the pupils the necessary intellectual equipment to think along the lines required for the task presented? The notion of learning readiness is recognised and accepted in the teaching of reading although some children may have to omit certain areas in the process of learning how to tackle unknown texts and words because of their particular problems. The concepts of *readability* and *reading age* are used together to ensure that pupils are able to cope with the books they are required to read. If, for example, a pupil with a reading age of 11 is faced with a book having a readability level of 14, frustration is the likely outcome. Reading ages can vary depending on the test used and, therefore, any measure that is gained from such tests must be treated cautiously. However, what such a measure will give is a pointer to the child's reading attainment. Some reading assessments (such as the Revised Neale or the MIRA or the NMRA assessment) give a reading band within which the pupil can be said to cope which makes matching books and texts somewhat easier.

Readability measures use a variety of formulae in order to calculate the difficulty of books or texts. Some can be worked out 'manually'; others can be found on computer programs. Once again the results of such measures should be treated with care as there is far more involved with the readability of books than a number score such as format, size of print, illustrations, subject matter etc.

It has now been acknowledged that the acquisition of spelling skills is also developmental although there are overlaps in these stages.

Teachers have to find out where pupils *are* and they have to involve the pupils in this process. Pupils have to learn self-assessment and also they have to realise that the inability to learn something may not have anything to do with lack of intelligence or diligence. Their problems may be the result of being inadequately prepared for a given learning task.

The idea of readiness is less often applied in other areas of study. Pre-testing to determine learning readiness is unfortunately a much under-used teaching technique. The child who gets lost and doesn't understand may be a victim of a system that does not include checks on learning readiness.

Closely related to the idea of learning readiness is the requirement that each pupil will need to *work at his or her own pace:* something not all that easy to organise and monitor in large classes.

A statement from a pupil, 'I can't do this, it is too hard,' presents a challenge to the teacher. The teacher has no choice but to agree with the pupil. If a task is seen as too hard by pupils, then either the subject matter itself, or the way it is expressed, is inappropriate for those pupils at that time. The next task is to establish why it is too difficult, and it is important that the pupils should take the fullest part in this exercise. The ultimate aim is that they should become wholly responsible for their learning and hence for identifying and overcoming difficulties for themselves.

Usually a difficulty results from gaps in knowledge, or lack of understanding of earlier steps in a sequential subject. It may be necessary to go back a long way to discover omissions or misunderstandings. It is useful to have prepared a task analysis, so that each piece of knowledge and each section of theory can be separately identified. Pupils can be presented with a check-list of all the things a learning-ready student should be expected to know and understand before tackling a particular topic, and asked to identify any areas of doubt or difficulty. When one of these areas has been selected, it may then be necessary to further analyse that item, in order to get to the root of the learning difficulty.

Task analysis

1. Write down, in sequence, all the steps necessary to carry out the task.

2. Make separate lists of the knowledge, skills and understanding required, *in terms of the things that the person carrying out the task must be able to do.*

3. Devise ways of assessing whether or not pupils have the necessary knowledge, skills and understanding to carry out the task, pre-testing. (This of course may not involve a formal testing. Probably, in practice, teachers will have a good idea of what a particular pupil knows, understands and can do. Pre-testing will be limited to those areas where the teachers, or the learners, are uncertain.)

4. Discuss the difficulties and dangers involved.
   The main point of task analysis is to discover precisely what subskills and knowledge are required for more complex tasks. It is possible, however, also to review the identified subskills in terms of difficulty and danger. For example, it may be difficult for some people to decide how much water to put into a kettle (enough to cover the element – not a lot more than is needed to avoid waste of electricity). It is obviously a potentially dangerous step to transfer boiling water from one place to another.
   To identify these is the first step in thinking about how to reduce the difficulties and ensure that suitable safety precautions are taken.

5. Think of ways to avoid or overcome them.

An example of task analysis

Making an apple pie

(This topic has been chosen because it represents a fairly common practical activity often undertaken with pupils who have special educational needs [as well as the majority of other children, it is to be hoped], and because, simple though the procedure is at first sight, it nevertheless provides a good opportunity to look at the procedures and benefits of task analysis. Exactly the same sort of procedure can be followed in all the subject areas at all levels of difficulty.)

(Previous task has been shopping for materials.)
1. Collect the materials required: apples, flour, salt, sugar, cooking fat.
2. Collect the cooking utensils needed: large basin, weighing machine, fork, tablespoon (tbs), teaspoon (tsp), pastry board, cutting board, rolling pin, blunt knife, sharp knife, peeler, baking tin, oven cloth.
3. Look up recipe.
4. Weigh out 8 ounces (230 grams) flour.
5. Transfer to large basin.
6. Add a pinch of salt.
7. Weigh out 8 ounces (230 grams) of cooking fat.
8. Transfer to basin with the flour and salt.
9. Work in the fat until the mixture resembles fine bread crumbs.
10. Add 3 tablespoons water.
11. Mix thoroughly using a fork or a knife.
12. Put some flour on the pastry board.
13. Transfer half the pastry dough to the pastry board.
14. Put some flour on top of the dough.
15. Roll out the dough to a circle just bigger than the pastry tin.
16. Place the round of pastry in the pastry tin.
17. Trim the edges with a blunt knife.
18. Take enough apples to fill the pie.
19. Peel the apples.
20. Cut the apples into pieces.
21. Remove the cores.
22. Slice the apples.
23. Arrange the slices in the pastry case.
24. Cover with sugar.

25. Sprinkle with a little water.
26. Roll out the other half of the pastry dough.
27. Moisten the edges of the dough in the pastry tin.
28. Cover the apples with the pastry top.
29. Press down the edges, using a fork.
30. Make two holes in the top of the pie, using a knife.
31. Place pie in the refrigerator for ten minutes.
32. Heat up the oven to gas mark 7 (220°C).
33. Place the pie in the oven, on the top shelf.
34. After 20 minutes check that the pie is cooking all right.
35. Look again from time to time until the pie is cooked as indicated by its colour.
36. Check that the apple inside is cooked by looking for bubbling juices.
37. Using an oven cloth, remove the cooked pie from the oven and place in a suitable place to cool.

Knowledge required
Able to recognise and name:
apples, flour, salt, sugar, cooking fat, large basin, kitchen scales, fork, tablespoon, teaspoon, pastry board, cutting board, rolling pin, blunt knife, sharp knife, peeler, baking tin, refrigerator, oven, parts of the oven (the temperature control, door, shelves), oven cloth.

Skills required
Can:
- read the recipe
- weigh
- 'work in' fat and flour
- fill a tablespoon with water
- transfer a spoon of water from one place to another
- manipulate a fork or knife adequately to mix pastry
- spread flour on a board
- roll out pastry
- transfer rolled out pastry to baking tin
- fit the pastry to the tin
- trim the edges of the pastry
- peel apples
- cut apples

- remove cores
- slice apples
- arrange apples in pastry case
- sprinkle sugar
- sprinkle water
- moisten edges of pastry
- use a fork to press down edges
- make suitable holes in the top of the pie
- set oven temperature
- use oven gloves correctly.

Understanding required
Can:
- follow the recipe
- use the scales correctly
- judge the degree of accuracy required
- judge a 'pinch' of salt
- 'work in' flour and fat
- recognise 'fine bread crumbs'
- spread a board with flour adequately
- estimate a 'half'
- estimate the number of apples to prepare
- use a suitable quantity of sugar
- decide how much water to add
- understand the need to fasten the top and bottom of the pie
- realise the danger of working with a hot oven
- see the relationship between the appearance of the cooking pie and its readiness
- distinguish between 'sharp' and 'blunt'.

Assessment of readiness
The *knowledge* items can be checked by asking children to bring things out of storage places and to set them on tables, or to respond to being asked to carry out instructions like 'open the oven door' or 'set the oven for gas mark 5'.

Most of the *skills* could be checked by observation on task, but some of them, involving an element of danger, would need to be separately assessed, namely the use of knives and working with the hot oven.

It is more difficult to check *understanding*. Most of the elements of understanding required for this particular task can be determined also by observation, because the task analysis breakdown sets out a series of operations which will only be correctly carried out if the pupils do understand what they are doing. This, however, would require careful observation of each pupil throughout the task, which would be difficult to do except with a very small group. It would, therefore, be sensible to carry out a discussion about any potentially difficult points. If pupils can explain concepts in their own words, it is likely that they have an understanding of them.

Looking for snags
The recipe. This, of course, is not in the form of the task analysis, which would (a) be far too long and (b) bear little relationship to any actual recipe a pupil might meet in a cookery book. Possible difficulties here are that the pupils may not be able to read it, or that they might not be able to interpret some of the terms or abbreviations within it. For example, would they be able to see the connection between 'tbs' and tablespoon, and would they be able to distinguish 'tbs' from 'tsp'? How would they cope if they were used to working with a gas mark for temperature indication and were faced with degrees C as for an electric oven? Again, suppose they had learnt to measure in ounces, but found the recipe to be expressed in grams?

The action to be taken would depend on the abilities of the pupils concerned. It might be helpful to present all instructions in diagrammatic form, which might provide sufficient backup following a demonstration, say. Or a cassette recording of instructions could be available.

'Working in the fat'. The traditional 'rubbing-in method' of working the fat into the flour is a rather messy operation, but seems to be favoured by most cooks. It would be sensible to regard this as an *advanced* skill and to teach instead a fork-mix technique, at least initially, for this recipe.

Using knives. Play safe with rather blunt ones. Teach good technique (both hands behind the blade) for *mastery* before working with any implement likely to cause an accident.

In response to the claim of a pupil that something is too difficult, a teacher ought to be able to reply with confidence, 'Yes, it is, but let us find out why. I know you can learn this!'

In the classroom teachers can help by:

- enabling pupils to discover where they are in terms of readiness for a particular learning task. Use of task analysis may be helpful here;

- enabling them to progress beyond it with or by means of a series of carefully modulated learning tasks, based on existing knowledge and abilities;

- providing successful learning experiences, thereby developing confidence;

- encouraging largely by means of justified praise.

Chapter 4 - Study skills in the classroom

The barriers referred to in Chapter 3 can affect greatly the way pupils cope with the curriculum areas and these should be kept in mind when deciding the best way to give appropriate study skill help. However, there are other reasons why pupils do not perform at their best in subjects or use adequate study skills. Study skills do not always come naturally. They can and ought to be taught.

Reading

In order to access most curriculum areas effectively pupils need to be able to read at least to a functional reading standard. This is either the standard at which books are written or at a reading level of around 9 years to 9 years 6 months which is thought of as the stage at which the reading fluency already gained will progressively develop with further practice.

Many children with special educational needs do not reach this level. Many who do are not able to use their reading skills effectively. Therefore, reading skills both have to be taught and developed. Too often textbooks and worksheets are written for a higher reading level than the pupil's reading attainment.

There are two main purposes in reading and they require different techniques. There is reading for pleasure and this includes reading novels and stories and poetry. There is also reading for information.

When reading for pleasure it is usual to read every word or nearly every word and it is often enjoyable to linger and reflect on the words and the thoughts they stimulate. When the pupils are encouraged to read for pleasure the teacher must ensure that the material provided is indeed capable of giving this favourable result. In order to achieve this, books should be able to sustain interest and should be within the readability of the pupil, at the pupil's particular level of reading attainment.

When reading for information, appropriate study skills are required for rapid access to that information. It is here that the so-called *'higher reading skills'* can be put into operation. This term is used not to imply that there is a 'hierarchy' of reading skills but to indicate that when a reader becomes fluent at a given reading level then other styles of reading can be brought into use.

Decoding has to become an automatic process before the skills of *skimming* and *scanning* can be employed. Skimming is otherwise known as rapid or speed reading. It means looking rapidly through a text in order to pick up the main ideas in it. Scanning means looking through a text for particular key words and ignoring everything else. In this way an entire book can be scanned to see if it contains any references to a topic under investigation. Reading for understanding is also very important especially where one has to read 'beyond' or 'between' the lines in order to decide on the author's meaning. There are some pupils who can cope with literal comprehension but have problems when having to be interpretative or to give their own ideas.

Pupils should know how to find their way around a library, how to use subject indexes and when to approach a librarian for help. Having a book to hand, they should know how to use tables of contents and chapter headings as well as the index itself as a means of determining content and assessing the worth of the book for any given task.

In the classroom teachers can help by:

- discussing and helping their pupils learn to recognise and read subject specific vocabulary in advance of meeting them in the subject context;

- referencing unusual words by using a pack of index cards to build a bank of words with their definitions;

- adapting worksheets etc. using shorter sentences and less complex words;

- checking readability by using one of the readability formulae to ensure that pupils can cope with the reading level required of them;

- encouraging guesswork;

- providing alternatives to reading such as using cassettes;

- setting questions in order to explore and help pupils' particular difficulties;

- demonstrating library methods for their own requirements, and thinking aloud before a class while doing so, or by asking appropriate questions of pupils engaged in library use;

- providing time trials to develop skimming skills: 'You have ten seconds to look at this page. Close your books, I'm going to ask you some questions';

- selecting particular words to develop scanning skills and seeing how many of these pupils find in a timed situation;

- setting questions on books based on the indexes, contents pages or chapter headings;

- setting group work on texts so that particular areas and questions are set for members of the group enabling collaborative learning to take place;

- encouraging the pupils to use their memories after reading starting with short passages and increasing these in length.

Spelling

Spelling is used for written communication and if the reader cannot read what the writer has written, communication does not take place. It is not the purpose of this book to talk about the teaching of spelling but to give some advice to teachers about how pupils can be encouraged to help themselves improve how they spell and to suggest some alternative procedures.

The actual process of acquiring spelling involves internalising the words. Pupils look at the word until they can as it were 'see' the word in the mind. Those pupils with very poor visual memories are at a disadvantage. So are those with poor auditory memories for using sounds for these may find memorising and using sounds a problem. Also they may find learning mnemonics as an aid to spelling words a difficult process. Learning a set of words to aid spelling retention can be more arduous and need more memory retention than remembering the actual word (e.g. IPSWICH = I Put Some Water In Charlie's Hat). Here the child has to remember the mnemonic and then extract the initial letter from each word in order to spell a seven letter word. Expecting children to learn a list of words for a test or to write out the words that were incorrect ten times each are negative activities, which is to say they are boring, destroying positive attitudes to work – and they don't work anyway!

In the classroom teachers can help by:

- encouraging pupils to try words in writing so that they can be shown what caused the difficulty and what part of the word was correct;

- encouraging pupils to identify spelling mistakes for themselves, by going through a piece of work and underlining words that do not look right. It is helpful to encourage this type of proof-reading but teachers should remember that pupils read their own work in order to take out the meaning and, therefore, because one can get meaning from incorrectly spelt words it is often difficult to find spelling mistakes. One way of checking work is to read it backwards and in that way words are read in isolation. However, this is a tedious activity and shouldn't be often used;

- asking other readers to be employed as markers (but take care with the sensitive pupils);

- reinforcing learning of spelling by expecting pupils to maintain a spelling dictionary, in which they write new words learnt. When a word has been used successfully three times without reference to the personal dictionary, then it may be crossed out as a word now mastered;

- discussing with the older learner that it is necessary to learn subject specific vocabulary. Teachers should not expect pupils to be able to spell such words. They must also ensure that the meaning is known;

- encouraging personal dictionaries as have been mentioned above for particular subjects and even using these as a thesaurus so that meanings are known and recorded or have sections within the dictionary for each subject;

- being aware that a visual process for learning to spell does not work for all learners and being also aware of their pupils' strengths and weaknesses in the process of learning to spell. It may be that they need different strategies. Examples of teaching points for older pupils are that where ordinary words are concerned help should be given with prefixes and suffixes, also it would be helpful for pupils to be shown the derivation of words and how words are built up from a root word (e.g. 'television' from 'tele' and words such as 'grace/graceful/gracefully/disgrace/disgraceful' etc.);

- stressing that the most important point for pupils is that because they are writing for an audience their work should be as legible and communicable as possible;

- encouraging and permitting the use of Spellcheckers and word processors;

- teaching pupils how to use these successfully;

- marking content (in terms of grading) not spellings but giving help with the spellings if the pupil wants this;

- allowing redrafting after the initial marking.

Written work

This can either come from note taking (see below) or from the pupils' own research. Often pupils with learning difficulties find it hard to know where to begin when they are asked to provide written work on any particular topic. Here brainstorming and mind-mapping can be used. Brainstorming is a term that normally refers to a group activity, but can be usefully applied to individual work as well. It is simply a matter of putting down as quickly as possible all ideas that occur to the participant about any topic to be considered. This produces a list which is a completely random collection of ideas associated with the topic, which can then be rearranged and accepted or rejected on the basis of further consideration. The great advantage of this activity is that it seems to free the mind from its normal constraints and allows for more creativity than a careful and systematic analysis in the first instance. This then, for some people, is a good way to begin any attempt at an article or an essay or a piece of literature.

Brainstorming will provide a repertoire of ideas. These should next be arranged in an order that is appropriate and makes sense. An inspection of this list will probably throw up other ideas, which can be added and also lead to an awareness of gaps to be filled or ideas for research and information to be sought. This in turn will lead to finding out more on certain topics, which may involve further thought, a visit to the library or some form of research. For those pupils who find it difficult to cope with a linear list it might be more helpful for them to mind-map. Each linked set of ideas is colour-coded or highlighted so that there is visual information to help the writer.

When all the information has been gathered and preliminary thinking and discussion has been completed, it is time to write a first draft. It should be noted that this is the point at which it has been traditional to begin. A teacher would say to a class, 'write a composition (or an essay or an account) of ...' and leave it to pupils to get on with it. The pupil's work was then examined, errors corrected and suggestions for improvement made. This other approach allows for influence to be available at a much earlier stage.

The first draft needs to be edited. This can profitably be a group activity, with pupils reading their work and inviting the comments of the group. Whether or not such an approach should be adopted depends very much on the nature and attitude of the group of pupils concerned and should never be attempted with the work of insecure children. Certainly at this point the teacher can make some suggestions, but the final arbiter should be the writers, who can seek the advice of their teachers and/or their peers, but should see it as advice rather than command. The pupils will then be expected to make a final revision and to write a final version. Obviously, access to a word processor could greatly facilitate this process as well as improve the motivation. However, pupils need competent word processing skills if this item of hardware is to be utilised successfully.

In the classroom teachers can help by:

- teaching pupils how to brainstorm ideas or organise solutions to a set problem where these are written as headings on a large sheet of paper and setting a given time for production;

- showing that alternative formats such as drawing boxes or having these drawn on a pro forma with the main paragraph section headings written in each box. In order to fill in the details a brainstorming session would then take place;

- helping pupils to group these keywords into areas. This could be done by using coloured pens to link the words but it is probably more effective for the group to 'cut and stick' so that the result is clear to see;

- allowing time and encouraging pupils to look for any 'gaps', further bits of information needed;

- encouraging the use of books for research depending upon the subject;

- helping to put these resultant sets of information or ideas into appropriate order (paragraphs);

- help with paraphrasing and making summaries by underlining or highlighting important words or by crossing out any information that seems unnecessary;

- showing how a first draft can be undertaken. It would be helpful for each member of the group to take one paragraph and write this;

- checking the finished product by encouraging others to verify and correct and add or delete until the group piece of work is completed;

- explaining the function of introduction and conclusion and the possible use of diagrams or pictures.

Essay writing

This is an addition to the above section on written work. Too often teachers expect that when a title has been given all pupils are able to write an essay which is well planned and interesting. The essay is marked after the event and mistakes are identified. Suggestions may be made as to how the essay might have been improved. However, essay writing is a skill that should be taught and the teaching should occur at an earlier stage in the essay writing process than is usually the case.

Below there are examples of webbing or mind-mapping because linear notes (see above) may not be easy for all pupils to follow. These pupils will need to brainstorm keywords or phrases and then link them by using boxes, numbers or coloured highlighter pens to show where there are similarities, subheadings or links with the main topic. Later it will be easier for these pupils to revise if they have used such aids.

Teachers will have to identify any lack of skills necessary for written work. These are the secretarial skills of handwriting, spelling and word processing. Pupils have to be able to organise their thoughts, and some of the ideas already given may help in this respect. Pupils should be able to proof-read their own and others' work and become markers and editors. This should be undertaken without fear of criticism, which means that the teacher must protect sensitive pupils from any possibility of mockery and that pupils must be allowed to opt out of such activity.

There are two types of writing, chronological and non-chronological, which require different activities (although not all these are essay-type activities). Jean Alston's book, *Assessing and Promoting Writing Skills* (NASEN, 1995) gives examples of these.

In the classroom teachers can help by:

- explaining the following technique: Some pupils would find it helpful to base their written work on a six (or more)-point plan. This could take the form of a spider diagram (see below) with the title written in the centre and whose legs make up the introduction and the conclusion. The other legs form the ideas which at its basic level would be each paragraph. This would help pupils understand the relevance of paragraphs as containing separate ideas or sections of information which are linked to each other;

- explaining the following technique: Instead of or following on from a spider, a ladder diagram (see below) could be drawn, where the top contains the title, the top rung the introduction and the bottom the conclusion with the other steps containing the linked paragraphs;

- providing the following ideas for both narrative stories and any essays which can be constructed by using questions. Examples of these are *who* did 'it', *what* was done, *where* did 'it' happen, *when* did 'it' occur, *why* did 'it' happen, in *which* way was 'it' done and *what* was the result. These questions may not be appropriate for every story or historical situation but by using them as headings the narrative could take shape;

- providing tactile and/or visual stimulus where and when appropriate;

- giving sentences and phrases which would provide some starting points;

- making use of modern facilitators like cassette-recorders or word processors;

- encourage proofreading (this is applicable for any type of written work). This should not necessarily be undertaken immediately after the work has been completed as it is more successful when done a day or two later;

- marking for content if spelling is a problem (this is applicable for any type of written work). This need not happen on every occasion but the pupil should be made aware when this is going to occur.

For essay/topic writing - Example a
Six (or more)-point plan
This is similar to the ideas given below but it forms an easier structure for those pupils who find it particularly difficult to write stories. Using this format a six-sentence story can be written or one of six paragraphs or even several pages.

1. characters (people)	2. location (place)	3. first part (what happens first)
4. second part (what happens next)	5. nearing the conclusion (what happens next)	6. conclusion (the end)

An example:
> Ben and his dog were on holiday.
> They went to the seaside.
> They went on the beach and heard a shout.
> Ben could see a girl up the cliff.
> His dog ran off to get help.
> The police saved the girl.

With discussion and questions this story became amplified into:

Ben went on holiday with his mum and dad. They took Kipper their dog with them. They went in the car.

They went to the seaside. It was a long way. Ben and Kipper were bored.

When they got to the seaside Ben and Kipper went on the beach. It was a sandy beach. The sea was blue. There were cliffs next to the beach. Ben and Kipper had a good time. Ben threw sticks to Kipper and Kipper ran into the sea. He got wet. Suddenly Ben heard a shout. It said 'Help.'

Ben said, 'What was that?' 'Help! Help!' said the shout. Ben looked round and he looked up the cliff. Ben saw a girl. She was stuck up the cliff. 'Help! Help!' she shouted.

Ben looked at Kipper. 'Run, Kipper. Go and get Dad.' Kipper ran off.

Soon Kipper came back with Dad and the police. The police climbed up the cliff and saved the girl. 'Thank you,' she said. 'Well done, Ben and Kipper,' said Dad.

Example b
Ladder diagram

Example c
Spider or web diagram

introduction

1st
paragraph

2nd
paragraph

3rd
paragraph

4th
paragraph

conclusion

introduction

idea   idea

TITLE
topic/heading

idea   idea

conclusion

There can be any number of paragraphs or ideas.
The introduction would be a sentence or two 'setting the scene' with a
similar number of sentences 'summing up' and forming the conclusion.
Each paragraph or idea would contain information that is similar or
relevant to the topic and each one would link to each other. A more
sophisticated way would be brainstorming as many ideas (words/phrases)
as can be thought of on the topic. These should then be grouped or
keywords would be listed under the paragraph headings.

Example d
Essay writing from a simple three-word sentence – a 'build a story' technique – where answers to directed questions can be turned into the introduction, the body and conclusion of the story.

- the dog barked

What sort of dog?
- an old brown Alsatian

How did it bark?
- loudly

Why did it bark?
- it heard a noise

What sort of noise?
- footsteps

Where did this happen?
- in a backyard

What was it like there?
- scary

Whose footsteps were they?
- a burglar's

What happened next?
- the dog chased the man

What happened in the end?
- the dog bit the man and stopped him running

How did they feel?
- the dog was pleased and the burglar was unhappy.

The complete story has become:
Bess, the old brown Alsatian, barked. She heard the sound of footsteps in the backyard. It was night-time and there were no stars or moon in the sky. A burglar was trying to break into the house. Bess chased the man and bit him. He stopped running and fell to the ground. Bess was pleased that she had caught him and the burglar was unhappy. It would be prison for him.

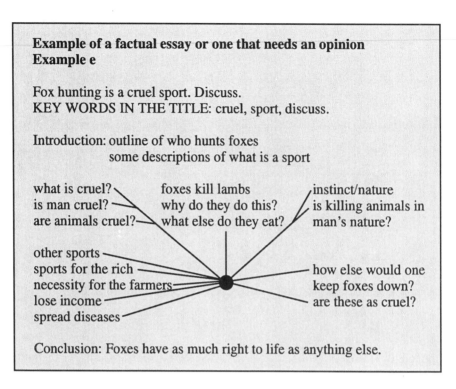

Example of a factual essay or one that needs an opinion
Example e

Fox hunting is a cruel sport. Discuss.
KEY WORDS IN THE TITLE: cruel, sport, discuss.

Introduction: outline of who hunts foxes
            some descriptions of what is a sport

what is cruel?   foxes kill lambs   instinct/nature
is man cruel?   why do they do this?   is killing animals in
are animals cruel?   what else do they eat?   man's nature?

other sports
sports for the rich   how else would one
necessity for the farmers   keep foxes down?
lose income   are these as cruel?
spread diseases

Conclusion: Foxes have as much right to life as anything else.

Note taking

Pupils are often expected to be able to cope with dictated notes, especially in the upper classes of the secondary school. In order to take notes well, pupils have to be able to hold information in their short-term memories and transfer the important or key words and phrases to paper. When notes are written successfully the substance of the lesson is recorded with the unimportant words left out. This is a skill which many adults find difficult and many try to write down verbatim what is being dictated. Therefore, unless the learner can write swiftly and legibly and can spell automatically, note taking will serve little purpose. It is possible to learn to write down the keywords but unless there is time at the end of the lesson for these to be enlarged they will probably mean very little when later read. Pupils have to learn how to pick out keywords and when they write these down they should be highlighted in some way, either by underlining or being boxed. Sometimes a drawing or representation could help. Also, when listening to information being given orally it is difficult to pick out what is relevant for later. Therefore, as an exercise note taking is not to be recommended although it is a skill which is still needed in certain circumstances. Linear note taking with clear headings is easier for the pupil to find the necessary information in the future.

If 'free' note taking is expected, as distinct from slow dictation (a technique not associated with interesting lessons) then the teacher should be aware of the relative importance of anything written on a chalkboard (or OHP) which would *certainly* be copied. Good structure and careful use of the chalkboard is essential if it is used in this way.

In the classroom teachers can help by:

- providing pupils with a copy of any information so that they are able to use it when making their own notes;

- providing a cassette-recorder or dictaphone so that the pupils can take notes for later analysis if the teacher demands that notes should be taken from a lecture-style lesson;

- allowing the pupils to have a copy of a friend's notes which could be helpful but only if these were legible and able to be understood;

- giving pupils the opportunity to ask questions during the lesson if notes are to be taken;

- discussing and permitting discussion of the subject that was being delivered in order that the pupils can gain any clarification necessary;

- giving out copies of hand-outs with key phrases on them as these would focus the pupils' attentions;

- giving keywords beforehand so that the pupils listen to these and add extra notes if necessary;

- using OHP transparencies which would serve a similar purpose;

- having information repeated and emphasised so that the pupils understand what items are relevant and so that the subject gets transferred into their working memories;

- giving linear notes with clear headings and subsection numbers in order to make information clearer.

Note making

Note *taking* means recording or transposing something already in existence. Essentially this is a mechanical process. Note *making,* on the other hand, involves a lot more mental effort and creativity. It involves understanding and structuring and selection. Very few people can do this in a single step.

Example of note making

The following information was dictated or read from a book or worksheet:
'Rain forests help to keep the world's weather from getting too hot. Heat from the rain forest is stored as water vapour. This water vapour rises up into the air high above the rain forest. When the water vapour gets to about 10 kilometres above the rain forest it changes into droplets of water. The heat that was stored moves into the air around the water vapour. Then this warm air moves towards the parts of the world that are cooler. Therefore, the rain forest's heat helps to warm some of the colder parts of the world. Because rain forests are being cut down there could be a change in the world's weather.'

As the words are being spoken or read the pupil should be able to jot down: 'rain forest heat stored as water vapour – up in air – 10 km water drops – heat into air – to cold countries – cut trees – change in world's weather.'

The above could be transcribed into the pupil's own words as:
'Heat from a rain forest is stored as water vapour. This rises up into the air. At about 10 kilometres it turns into drops of water and the stored heat goes into the air. This heat goes to colder countries. If we cut down the trees in the rain forests there could be a change in the world's weather.'

Many of us find it necessary to jot down rough notes and then go over them at a later time, reorganising and supplementing them as necessary. At its simplest level this may be involved in preparing the minutes of a meeting. In the learning process it is an extremely important study skill, and one that ought to be positively and actively taught rather than left to chance.

It is a skill that older pupils are often expected to be able to cope with and one that is rarely taught. Pupils sometimes resist attempts to get them to become note makers. Conscientious and timid pupils may lack the confidence to make their own notes and would much prefer to take down a set produced by the teacher.

In the classroom teachers can help by:

- talking over facts before the pupils have to take notes or produce written work;

- giving the learner the opportunity to write down key words and phrases immediately after such a note-taking lesson has taken place;

- organising group work as this would give the opportunity for all important items to be remembered;

- teaching pupils that these key items should be grouped into clusters so that all the information becomes a *web* with branches from the centrally placed main subject heading. Using this principle of *webbing* individual note taking from either heard or read information can take place (see section on essay writing);

- providing a timer so that the learner is restricted to what can be recalled in a specified length of time, say 5 minutes at the maximum, in order to help pupils brainstorm their knowledge in words and phrases;

- making notes readily accessible for the learner by producing a wall chart as a visual source of gathered information. This would be helpful for revision purposes.

Projects

Generally pupils regard a project as a gathering of information. Quite reasonably they may consider that the author of a printed book can probably express ideas better than they can. Hence, most pupils in those subjects where projects may be undertaken see these as exercises in copying out of books or cutting and sticking pictures rather than having to undertake any individual research. This is often because pupils are not helped to acquire the skills of project making. If possible they should be given the opportunity of making a personal choice of topics. To do this they have to be able to ask questions, to make their own decisions, to be aware of alternatives. They have to know the areas of knowledge relevant to their particular chosen topic; they have to decide what questions should be asked and what information should be researched and what sources of information they should use. Decisions have to be made about selecting sources that are

45

relevant and knowing where to find these. Some pupils may try to use too much information and, therefore, become dispirited about the amount to be looked for and read. On the other hand most research demands more than one source of information, so that a balance has to be struck. For a child with special educational needs this can be a challenging undertaking.

First the pupil has to undertake research for the project and in this section there are references to reading and allied skills which are dealt with elsewhere. Added to these the pupils have to learn how to recognise which information is relevant to the questions that they need to pose and then answer. When books with diagrams and pictures are used, the pupils need adequate observation skills so that they are able to use this additional evidence.

Next comes the organisation of information relevant to the project which is a very important skill. The pupils must learn to arrange information and ideas in an appropriate sequence. This could be summarised into the acquisition of organising skills of:

- classifying

- ordering

- analysing

- synthesising.

The project then has to be expressed in some form and not every project or essay needs to be written in its entirety. There are a variety of ways of expressing information and ideas and these need to be selected as to which would be most appropriate ways.

Examples of these are:

- drawing diagrams

- painting or sketching

- model making

- map making

- cassette recording

- word processing.

There are also non-written or non-visual ways of getting ideas across but mostly these cannot be stored or kept. Examples of these are anything which could be termed dramatic and which involve discussion, debate or reporting verbally.

At the completion of the project the work has to be evaluated, as any work undertaken needs an audience and pupils should not be content to allow solely their teachers to mark or judge their work. Self-evaluation is important as can be peer-evaluation. Pupils must look back to the questions asked at the beginning of the work, at the initial drafts and judge how adequate is the final result in relation to these.

Example
A project is an extended investigation that might involve a considerable range of learning experiences including library work, experimental work, IT etc. A project on the *physics of sound* could include looking up books on musical instruments, making musical instruments and investigating ways of altering pitch or loudness, learning about vibrations and the way they travel.

Each pupil would be required to produce a folder of material, which would include a complete record of the work carried out, and possibly a cassette recording of sounds produced under different conditions.

In the classroom teachers can help by:

- guiding the pupils' choice of questions;

- knowing how to add to these first questions, if necessary, in order to ensure that the pupils look at their area more widely;

- knowing the pupils well enough to be able to give them advice as to how much work they should undertake;

- being aware of the resources that are needed and where these are located.

Information seeking

These are the important skills needed for project and research work. Many children take a delight in gathering information and preparing projects. There are many sources of information although it is increasingly the practice to provide work and information for pupils in the form of worksheets. These can facilitate the organisation of individual work and can be provided at different ability levels, but there are dangers in this. If such an approach is to be adopted then it is important that the core material is provided at a basic level, this means at a level that every member of the class can understand, backed up if necessary by pictures or cassette/video recordings. Extension material can be provided at any appropriate level, but teachers should make sure that the more able do not get or be seen to be getting all the fun. Teachers must be aware also that they may be providing more practice and consolidation for those who need it least. Worksheets should frequently be reviewed for:

- legibility

- readability

- language content.

The same should occur with text books and these also should be reviewed for their conceptual level.

In the classroom teachers can help by:

- making sure that materials provided are differentiated;

- checking that worksheets are well written, legible and good to look at. They should also be at the correct readability level for their particular audience;

- making sure that the text books used contain correct information, are able to be read and understood by their audience and that their language content is at the correct level;

- giving information in different formats.

Expressing ideas

Traditional teaching employs as a matter of course the asking of questions. These are addressed to the class as a whole and an oral response is expected. This is a way by which a teacher can gauge the degree of understanding of his or her class. It is also a means of requiring attention and participation. This teaching strategy is sometimes regarded as *discussion,* as a way of enabling pupils to express their ideas, but this is very seldom the case in practice, especially when 'closed' questions as distinct from open-ended ones are asked.

Examples

Closed questions (questions to which there is only one answer – the one in the mind of the teacher).
What is the capital of France?
What is 6 x 6?
What colour do you get when you mix yellow and blue paints?

Open questions (questions to which there are several possible answers).
What is your favourite food?
How could we measure the length of the playground?
Where would you like to go for a holiday?

So how are pupils to be helped to learn to express themselves orally? Do they need help in this respect, or is it not a skill that comes naturally? Few of us like to risk ridicule in a large group. It takes a special kind of courage and confidence to speak from the floor at a large meeting of one's peers.

In the classroom teachers can help by:

• encouraging discussion first between pairs of pupils and in small groups before whole classwork. Pupils under such conditions will learn naturally and discover just how difficult it is to communicate ideas by means of words. They will know when they have succeeded immediately by the response of their partner or the group. It is difficult to monitor such classroom procedures and difficult to assess progress, but use of group discussions is undoubtedly an important teaching procedure;

- giving pupils props, either keywords or short phrases or even a picture or an artefact, that will help them with their expressive ideas;

- letting the pupils know beforehand what they will be expected to discuss so that they have time to marshal their thoughts and to practice;

- giving those pupils who feel discussion to be particularly difficult some time individually so that they gain in confidence.

Beyond learning to creativity

Creativity is difficult to define, but it is usually possible to recognise its results. It is associated with imagination, originality and intuition. It can be seen in a divergent thinker who tackles problems and issues from an imaginative and original standpoint. Creative learners may take risks and be seen as different from their peers by their peers and their teachers. Creativity may be impossible to teach, but at least it may be recognised and encouraged. The teacher will want to provide opportunities for it to occur. Originality is one feature of creativity, but associated with it in practice are other qualities like enthusiasm, persistence, prolificacy, synthesis and intelligence. Teaching for creativity is in the realm of process.

Teachers will need to be aware of under what conditions creativity is most likely to occur. If these can be set out then they define the process which should be adopted.

In the classroom teachers can help by:

- giving a high priority to original work;

- recognising and praising imaginative work whenever it occurs;

- using open-ended questions and adopting problem-solving approaches.

Mathematics

Mathematics is an example of a sequential subject although not wholly so. Its content and concepts can be arranged in an optimum learning order but concepts are also formed by generalising from a variety of perceptual experiences. However, it is often taught in a fragmented way so that pupils find it difficult to see the links between areas. It is also a subject virtually free of redundant information if processes are given as sums. In reading, or indeed any subject that involves reading, lots of words could be missed out and the sense would survive. As we read a book, it is usual to find a great deal of repetition, which serves to reinforce and establish our understanding of the topic. If, on the other hand, a single step is missed out in a mathematical process or some other aspect of mathematics, all is lost. It would be like a faulty computer programme, one in which a step was missing. However, a mathematical problem taken from a real life situation can be full of redundant information so that the problem solver has to sort out the relevant from the irrelevant in order to determine what answer is required and what elements have to be processed in order to find it.

If pupils find themselves *lost* at some stage, the reason for the difficulty can lie far back in their mathematical experience, something needed now which was missed out earlier on. When this sort of experience has been repeated again and again over the years, then confidence can be reduced to zero, mathematics becomes a *mystery* and genuinely hated.

In the classroom teachers can help by:

- helping the pupils to begin to analyse, preferably with the help of one who has mastered the topic, just what is missing in the necessary sequence of understanding to remedy the problem;

- breaking down the task into small steps as in task analysis as this procedure will be found invaluable in this respect;

- looking at the way pupils can use their own learning and own strategies and go on from there.

Rote learning

This may be facilitated sometimes by understanding, but there is a large amount of factual knowledge of a kind that requires no understanding (which could be found in books or computer data bases) which is generally regarded as necessary for an educated person to carry in the memory. Historical dates, names of places and *general knowledge* are in this category. So too are the number facts, for, although they are based on experience (and best taught through the use of concrete materials) and although they can be 'worked out' by counting on fingers or 'adding on' etc., in order to be useful they must simply be remembered without any thought, as facts.

Rote learning seems to be largely a matter of repetition, but the nature of the repetition does matter, and some children adopt unhelpful but still time-consuming methods. Many children think that if they simply read through a passage or their notes a number of times then eventually they will memorise the facts concerned. Learning tables is a poor way of learning the number facts. One reason is that tables can be made by simply adding on, which might be good practice at the process of adding, but does not contribute much to the memorising of the actual *products*. Another effect of chanting tables is that the facts within them can come to seem unmanageable and in daunting quantity.

In the classroom teachers can help by:

- using the following set of stages. (Although these are for number facts they can be adapted for other memory work.)

  a) Pupils should be shown that the best way to learn number facts, and most other facts that are to be memorised, is to write them individually on pieces of card, with a question on one side and the answer on the other.

  b) These cards should then be placed in a convenient container and drawn out at random.

  c) An answer should be required immediately, with no hesitation, as this would allow for thinking. What is required is instant recall, mastery of the facts and not a demonstration of the ability to work them out or even of understanding.

  d) It is as well to start with only about three of these facts.

---

e) They should be memorised by inspection first and then the success or otherwise of the process tested by taking out the cards, offering an answer and then immediately checking. (This also provides a way to involve the family, because it is better, but not essential, that someone else takes out the cards and poses the questions.)

f) It can be operated in the spirit of a game and provides plenty of opportunities for providing rewards of all kinds.

g) About three facts can be learnt in a day and another three cards are added each day. There are only about 70 number facts in the whole of mathematics, including all the number bonds and products (see *The Third R Towards a Numerate Society*, ed. Glenn, 1978). At three a day, therefore, a child can become what is usually regarded as numerate in just over three weeks! It works.

There still remain to be taught the processes of mathematics and their applications, but these become appreciably easier given the confidence provided by the attainment of numeracy.

Information technology

There are many ways in which information technology (IT) can be used to enhance and support pupils' learning. For some pupils access to specific technology can act as a strongly motivating factor; for others it is a tool which can be used to support and develop particular aspects of the pupils' work and learning skills. Certain features of IT allow pupils immediate feedback about their work. This gives them the opportunity to amend what they are doing and gain a degree of learning autonomy. As with all resources used to support learning it is necessary to evaluate the features that a piece of equipment can offer and match these to an individual pupil's needs.

In the classroom teachers can help by:

- allowing pupils access to a range of IT resources: computers, handheld spellcheckers, concept keyboards, calculators etc.;

- being familiar with features of the programs and matching these to pupils' needs;

- evaluating the resources critically (for example, with programs that teach specific skills are the penalties more attractive than the rewards? is it possible to vary the speed of presentation of items? how many errors and what kind of errors does a spellchecker pick up?);

- encouraging pupils to be confident and independent when using IT and developing pupils' familiarity with the basic functions of the computer;

- teaching basic keyboarding skills;

- using computers' speech facilities to increase the efficacy of spellcheckers and enhance pupils' independence;

- creating subject specific word banks for the pupils to use;

- teaching pupils how to draft and edit on screen;

- using programs which are specifically designed to allow pupils to organise their thoughts and ideas (brainstorming on computer);

- using concept keyboards to help pupils develop sequencing skills; to use word banks or teach specific letter strings;

- using graphic programs which include templates for pupils with poor motor skills;

- encouraging the pupils to experiment with different fonts etc.

Chapter 5 - Organisational and self-help skills

Learning doesn't just occur in the classroom. It may start there but be completed within the home as homework. Therefore, ultimately learning has to become self-directed. When homework is given it will usually need organisational skills for its effective completion. Children also need to be able to organise their own social and working lives. They live within family cultures where as individuals they have to fit in with others. Those children who find it very hard to remember and recall do not just find life difficult for themselves – they can make life difficult for others. It is in everyone's best interests that everyone has acceptable organisational and self-help skills.

Effective learning

What works for one person may not do so for another. It is, therefore, not possible for teachers (or parents) to be prescriptive, but a range of options and examples can be provided and pupils can be encouraged to try them out for themselves and to determine which works best for them. Working effectively means learning as much as possible in a given time. It means choosing the shortest route to a particular end and avoiding distractions on the way.

The concept of *time on task* is a useful one in this context. Unsuccessful school pupils are the ones who only work when the teacher is standing over them. Under such conditions or with such poor motivation a pupil may only *work* one or two minutes in an hour.

Ineffective work is either a pretence of work, such as reading words without understanding and internalising the sense of them, or it is misdirected. The task of the teacher here is first to recognise the possibility of the former and discourage it, and to help pupils avoid the latter. This in many cases ties in with the notion of *learning readiness,* as pupils are much more likely to go off on a false path or at a tangent if they are not really ready for the planned learning experience, or have little idea of the purpose of the learning task concerned.

Teachers or parents can help by:

- setting objectives (see below);

- helping the pupils to work out their own rates and lengths of learning. Here the pupils learn how to develop time management techniques. At home parents should see that their children have somewhere to work which is congenial and where interruptions are kept to the minimum;

- rewarding increasing time on task rather than just task completion.

Setting objectives

It often helps to set objectives, to have a clear idea of just what should be achieved in a particular learning session. Here again general teaching practice seldom provides a good example. It is relatively rare for pupils to be in possession of a syllabus of what is being studied or to be given either the long-term aims or short-term objectives of a particular course of lessons. Most children have very little idea of what is going to happen in any particular lesson until they get there. If they are to be fully involved in their learning they might be told, for example, 'At the end of this lesson you should be able to ...' or 'today we are going to practise ... in order to reinforce ...'

Teachers can help by:

- providing pupils with a list of course content, possibly in the form of objectives;

- stating clearly at the beginning of each lesson the area to be covered and the content to be learnt during that period. If pupils can see the overall plan of their studies they are more likely to see the point of them and to appreciate how they can contribute to the learning process.

Self-assessment

Pupils should be encouraged to assess their own learning and progress. This is, in fact, one of the most important aspects of learning to learn. It is part of taking responsibility for learning. Pupils should reach a stage where teacher-based assessment is a formality, because the pupils have already tested themselves and know whether or not they have attained their objectives, whether or not they have memorised something or understood something.

Too often pupils regard tests and testing with something approaching dread. Pupils should be encouraged to regard any tests as something of use to them to provide them with a greater understanding of their learning progress and attainment.

Teachers can help by:

- providing pupils with the insight into self-assessment so that they are able to match their learning to the outlined objectives;

- treating in-school tests and examinations as positive activities and not demeaning pupils for poor results but helping them to understand where they had difficulties;

- balancing normative with criterion-referenced assessments which show pupils' progress is still developing;

- developing Records of Achievement.

Planning and checking work

As pupils grow older they need to be able to plan their work effectively and to check that they have successfully completed their objectives. This should take place both for classwork and under examination conditions. It is becoming more common for schools to request extra time in examinations for those pupils who it is felt would benefit from this. This is particularly so in the case of pupils with a specific learning difficulty. However, this extra amount of time has to be used wisely. It is often tempting for young people to start writing immediately rather than spending time thinking and planning. Much of what has been written about note making and essay writing comes into play here. Pupils should mind-map or make web diagrams before they begin any piece of work. An initial plan with logically sequenced steps can be referred to throughout the piece of writing and the points ticked off when completed.

There should also be time set aside for checking work. In non-examination conditions this is easier because the pupil will feel under no time restraints and course work should be checked the next day. If this happens the pupil will re-read the work afresh. Under examination conditions there may only be time to read to see if all the points have been entered and if the work makes sense.

Teachers can help by:

• giving pupils guidance on how to plan by dividing the allotted time constructively;

• making sure they know about the techniques for webbing etc.;

• explaining that it may help to underline keywords on the examination paper or scribble points over this;

• making sure that they can write clearly with the points stated simply;

• giving help on re-reading and checking techniques.

Assessment (in-school and external)

From the point of view of the learners, the main value of assessment is to provide independent feedback on their learning. However, it should be queried whether pupils get to know the result of their efforts soon enough to look back and note what they did that caused it to be correct or incorrect.

Some forms of assessment, namely the norm referenced kind, designed to arrange people in order of ability, can have an extremely negative effect on the learner. If learners are placed in a lower group because of how they fared in a particular assessment, they may have a lower opinion of their abilities and will not expect to do well. This sort of streaming, or setting system, is damaging to self-confidence, to self-esteem and to enthusiasm.

If pupils with learning difficulties have some particular problem with the way they are able to tackle some part of the assessment process then they will not perform at their best. Examination boards are at present allowing some pupils to have their papers dictated to them, to use alternative means of recording, to be allowed an amanuensis (scribe) or to be given extra time. In-school assessments can grant any help that can be organised but for external examinations a current educational psychologist's report is necessary and schools will have to negotiate with examination boards.

Teachers can help by:

- using a system of criterion-referenced testing, based on a set of learning objectives;

- making these objectives available to the pupils themselves ('at the end of this section you will be able to ...');

- being careful not to constantly reinforce pupils' notions of their own low abilities;

- being aware of particular children's needs and arranging the correct ways of helping them to meet their potentials.

Revising

There are two kinds of revision. The most obvious one is the one which is part of the preparation people carry out prior to examinations. The other more important aspect, which indeed could almost obviate the need for examination revision, is an ongoing consolidation of what is being learnt. This latter is constantly practised in non-sequential subjects, like English and art, but is at least as important in more structured subjects like mathematics and the sciences. Learners should keep a revision notebook going all the time they are learning. This is not only going to become invaluable for efficient revision as an examination approaches, but also provides a useful way of consolidating knowledge gained. Those who simply make a copy of whatever is in their notes or from a textbook are probably not processing and internalising the material at all and are practising an activity which above all is the antithesis of learning skill, fooling themselves that since they are putting in the time and producing something, then they are actually learning.

Teachers and parents can help by:

- giving hints on revision techniques:

  - deciding where to revise

  - deciding what area in the subject will be covered for the examination or test

  - deciding what is most likely to be asked

  - deciding what should be remembered and what may be able to be worked out during the assessment

  - deciding what is the learner's best learning strategy. This could be dictating information on a cassette or making diagrams, lists or keywords or reading information out loud

  - deciding which books etc. are needed for studying

  - deciding how much time should be allocated for studying

  - deciding how to self-test;

- providing a suitable small notebook for revision purposes and monitoring the way this is used throughout a course of study;

- asking questions and discussing various aspects of lessons so that the pupil can continue ongoing learning.

Examination techniques

Examinations do not have much to do with the process of learning. They are used within the education system to check how much the child has retained from particular subjects and how much he or she can use former acquired knowledge. In order to cope with examinations, the candidate must first learn to read and interpret the questions. Under examination conditions, nervous and concerned, questions and the rubrics which precede them are frequently misread.

Teachers can help by:

- encouraging relaxation;

- helping with how to plan and how to allocate plenty of time to read the paper and to read it again to ensure that no marks are needlessly lost through what is called carelessness, but might be better attributed to caring too much, if in the wrong way;

- helping the pupils in the process of interpreting the questions. Questions can be ambiguous and/or ill-expressed, and a candidate has to be able to recognise what is in the mind of the examiner, what is wanted as distinct from what the words of the question seem to imply;

- giving some guidance in interpreting the printing of the mark allocation which is to be found alongside the question. As a general rule, for example, if five marks are allocated for a part of a question then something like five points will be expected in the answer. The mark allocation does give some indication of the length of response expected, and may rule out some more extended explanation, say, or a one-word answer;

- helping the candidates to plan the allocation of time. Candidates frequently lose marks because they have failed to complete a paper. The rubric to the exam may give some guidance as to the amount of time that should be spent on any section of the paper, but the candidate must do his or her mathematics carefully and ensure that time has been allowed for reading over the question paper and for looking over the paper before handing it in, prior to deciding how long to spend on each question;

- explaining that if time is running out it may be sensible to indicate in some way such as by a web or linear diagram that information is actually known about the last unanswered question;

- explaining that unless it is stated otherwise the questions can be answered in any order;

- spending time going through examples of examination rubrics and making sure they are fully understood;

- going through with a class several sample examination papers solely for the purpose of establishing good technique, giving examples of the interpretation of questions, of appropriate lengths for answers and so on.

Taking a break

As there is a limit to how long anyone can concentrate when revising or studying, students need to know their optimum study time and to take rests in order to avoid mental fatigue. Most experienced workers know when they have reached the limit of their concentration, when the mind begins to wander, when they begin to make mistakes or when a word sought refuses to come to mind. At such point it is useless to go on. This is the time when adult workers go for a coffee, or do something quite different, either something mechanical or listening to music or practising relaxation. It is seldom that schoolchildren are either given an opportunity to determine their own work patterns like this, still less are they instructed in such an approach. School pupils are expected to do their time-out sessions between periods or during breaks and are accused of being lazy or inattentive if discovered switching off for themselves during lessons. Learning to work effectively is of importance to all pupils, for all pupils in mainstream schools are faced with examinations and, therefore, revision. In particular pupils with specific learning difficulties often find it hard to organise their revision time.

Teachers and parents can help by:

- encouraging pupils when learning to work effectively to know when not to work or when to take a break. At home all pupils must determine for themselves how long they can work effectively at a stretch, what to do to take a break which is refreshing and relaxing, and how long that break should be;

- being guided about effective working at home. When homework is given there is little help about how to tackle it. Many pupils find it hard to organise their evenings so that they can both relax and study. Much homework is crammed into a bus ride to school or some minutes at the breakfast table;

- providing wherever possible a place for children to study which is free from interruptions, pleasant and warm either in school or at home;

- encouraging their children to do their homework at the same time each evening and for the same amount of time. Children with organisational difficulties might easily procrastinate if they had to choose when they would study;

- helping them as they grow older to organise their own learning and studying. This is of particular importance if they transfer to further education. There has to be a routine for private study, whether this is at school, college or home;

- advising that the following routine should be suggested. A given amount of time (and this would depend on each pupil) such as 10 minutes could be spent revising any previous work, 30 minutes for working on new or difficult work and another 10 minutes to go over any notes that have been made or to make a check on what has been learned. A break every 50 minutes is sensible and for some children this will need to be more frequent. At this time there could be time for a short walk around or a drink. It is advisable not to use that time for watching TV as this could either interrupt or stop work altogether;

- being careful about stopping their children learning with music in the background. For some this can be soothing and helpful.

Organisation

Once pupils have taken responsibility for their own learning, they should then be encouraged to organise their learning. This is about adjusting to independence or overcoming dependence on teachers or other adults. The ultimate form of this would reduce the teacher to one of many resources, to be made use of by the pupils. To be rather more realistic, the teacher would add to this minimal role those of mentor and counsellor, or director of studies. Pupils will turn to that teacher whenever they are unable to analyse for themselves any particular learning difficulty for help in identifying the source of the problem. They will look to their teacher to provide support and encouragement. They will look to the teacher as an inspiration, as a source of interest and enthusiasm, from whom they will possibly have caught the desire to learn in the first place. One of the problems that pupils might have is in organising time, especially when they are working on homework or revision. Some pupils find it difficult to plan ahead as they have little conception about the passage of time and how long it will take them to complete anything. They will need help in getting started with work but this will have to be organised realistically, taking into account the habits of the pupil.

Teachers and parents can help by:

- providing those pupils with organisational difficulties with several copies of their own timetables and displaying these or keeping these in different places. Many pupils become very worried if they think that they will forget where they should be;

- suggesting that pupils could keep a reference notebook for all new learnt structures like a daily diary;

- helping the pupils keep their work neat, tidy and in order by providing ring files and coloured dividers with a contents list for organising subjects. This is because most pupils in secondary schools have no storage units so they carry their work around in large bags. If they have organisational problems they do not dare to leave anything at home in case they forget something so their personal and school belongings are dragged around from home to school and class to class;

- providing wall planners either in their children's bedrooms or the kitchen which would give daily reminders of what is needed for the next day or the next week;

- helping their children to learn to check at the same time each day;

- making a checklist of the correct equipment needed for any particular lesson;

- putting name tags on losable items;

- suggesting that pupils divide their homework and/or revision time into blocks of around 40 minutes as this length of time is appropriate before concentration levels start to fall;

- helping to organise the week into realistic work blocks.

Conclusion

Most teachers present their subjects with flair and enthusiasm. They provide notes when appropriate, and they monitor pupil progress through regular assessment and countless hours of marking. They like and respect their pupils and wish them well in all respects.

Parents try to provide what is necessary to enable their children to grow into competent and well-adjusted adults.

Many pupil attitudes are determined by social circumstances rather than by what happens within schools. Attitudes are a product of pupils' own dispositions, social circumstances and school experiences. We do believe, however, that schools, by adopting an approach designed to help children to learn for themselves, will maximise the possibility that when pupils have forgotten all they learnt at school they will find themselves able and equipped to go on learning for themselves should they want to. For well-motivated pupils with special needs, the prime requirement is to develop independence. To maximise the degree of independence in learning, it is necessary for pupils to have independent learning skills. It is towards such pupils that this booklet is aimed and we hope that, by learning to learn, they will also gain in confidence and be better able to cope with the world in general.

References

Ainscow, M and Tweddle D (1988) *Encouraging Classroom Success,* Fulton, London.

Alston, J (1995) *Assessing and Promoting Writing Skills New Edition,* NASEN, Tamworth.

Barthorpe, T and Visser, J (1991) *Differentiation: Your Responsibility,* NASEN, Tamworth.

Code of Practice on the Identification and Assessment of Special Educational Needs (1994), DfE, London.

Education Act (1993), HMSO, London.

Education Act (1988) *The Education Reform Act,* HMSO, London.

Rousseau, J (1762) *Emile au de l'education.*

Science in the National Curriculum (1995), HMSO, London.

Glenn, J (1978) (Editor) *The Third R Towards a Numerate Society,* Harper and Row, London.

Neale, M. Neale Analysis of Reading Ability. NFER-Nelson, Windsor.

Selmes, I (1987) *Improving Study Skills,* Hodder and Stoughton, London.

Vincent, D and de la Mare, M. Individual Reading Analysis, NFER-Nelson, Windsor.

Vincent, D and de la Mare, M. New Reading Analysis, NFER-Nelson, Windsor.

Visser, J (1993) *Differentiation: Making It Work,* NASEN, Tamworth.